Calligraphy Meets Philosophy

Talk 3

尚語

第三話

KS Vincent POON（潘君尚）

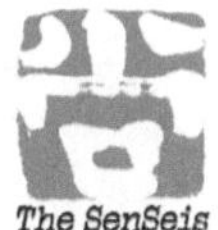

First Edition
Aug 2024

Published by
The SenSeis 尚尚齋
Toronto
Canada
www.thesenseis.com
publishing@thesenseis.com

ISBN 978-1-989485-34-7

Cover
Honinbo Doetsu's Go Board
Mitsui Memorial Museum
本因坊道悦舊藏碁盤
三井記念美術館
Tokyo Japan

In Loving Memory of My Beloved Mother

Pui Luen Nora TSANG（曾佩鑾）

Table of Contents

Li Qingzhao, *A Quatrain Written in a Summer* (李清照《夏日絕句》)

A Phrase From *Analects – Xue Er* (《論語•學而》句)

Sima Guang, *The Family Precepts of Sima Guang* (司馬光《司馬溫公家訓》)

A Phrase From *A Narrative on Calligraphy* (《書譜》句)

A Phrase From *New Book of Tang – Comments on the Biography of Yan Zhenqing* (《新唐書•顏真卿傳贊》句)

Calligraphy Meets Philosophy - Talk 3

Introduction

(I)

The *Calligraphy Meets Philosophy* series aims to foster a correct and deeper understanding of traditional Chinese calligraphy and philosophy. It does so by having calligraphies of selected classical texts accompanied by line-by-line translations and annotated remarks.

(II)

Talk 3 focuses on outlining some important traditional Chinese concepts like "Filial Piety (孝)", "Wisdom (智)", "Tacit Deeds of Grace (陰德)", and "Cultivating One's Foundations (務本)", etc... Selected texts include those by Bai Juyi (白居易, 772-846 AD), Liu Yuxi (劉禹錫, 772-842 AD), Li Qingzhao (李清照, 1084-1151 AD), Sima Guang (司馬光, 1019-1086 AD), Sun Guoting (孫過庭, 648-703 AD), and Sun Yat-Sen (孫逸仙, 1866-1925); as well, phrases from the canonical *Analects* (《論語》), *Book of Rites* (《禮記》), and *Platform Sutra* (《六祖壇經》) are also included. The book concludes with KS Vincent Poon's modelling and remarks on the Chinese calligraphy masterpiece *Yi Ying Stele* (《乙瑛碑》).

(III)

Here, I would like to thank my father, Dr Kwok Kin POON (潘國鍵博士), for his enduring assistance. His invaluable insight on correctly interpreting various old texts has contributed significantly to my translations. Further, his continuing encouragement has always been the source of my passion. Perhaps this is a prime example of "passing on (傳承) the family's profession and reputation (家業)", a custom that the Japanese hold so dearly. And that is exactly why Japan can still retain its traditional culture and values.

KS Vincent Poon
August 2024, Toronto

Bai Juyi
A Poem for the Swallows

白居易
《燕詩》

Calligraphy

Calligrapher (書者): KS Vincent Poon (潘君尚)

Content (內容): *A Poem for the Swallows,* a poem by Bai Juyi (白居易《燕詩》)

Style (字體): Standard Script (楷書)

Caption (款識): 白居易燕詩丁酉冬潘君尚 (Bai Juyi *A Poem for the Swallows,* during winter in the year of the Dingyou, Kwan Sheung Vincent Poon)

Seal Inscription (鈐印): 君尚 (朱文) (Kwan Sheung Vincent, red characters), 潘氏 (白文) (The Surname of Poon, white characters)

Medium (材料): Ink on Xuan paper (紙墨水本)

Size (尺寸): 75 X 35cm

Year (年份): 2017

梁上有雙燕　翩翩雄與雌　銜泥兩椽間　一巢生四兒
四兒日夜長　索食聲孜孜　青蟲不易捕　黃口無飽期
嘴爪雖欲敝　心力不知疲　須臾十來往　猶恐巢中飢
辛勤三十日　母瘦雛漸肥　喃喃教言語　一一刷毛衣
一旦羽翼長　引上庭樹枝　舉翅不回顧　隨風四散飛
雌雄空中鳴　聲盡呼不歸　卻入空巢裏　啁啾終夜悲
燕燕爾勿悲　爾當反自思　思爾為雛日　高飛背母時
當時父母念　今日爾應知

白居易燕詩　丁酉冬　潘君尚

Translation

白居易 《燕詩》
Bai Juyi, *A Poem for the Swallows*

1. 梁上有雙燕 ,
Two swallows were upon a wooden beam,

2. 翩翩雄與雌。
A he and a she stood elegantly (翩翩) as a team.

3. 銜泥兩椽間 ,
Clays amassed by their beaks (銜泥) rested between two wooden pilings,

4. 一巢生四兒。
A nest that hatched four offspring.

5. 四兒日夜長 ,
The four offspring grew by the day and night,

6. 索食聲孜孜。
Demanding food endlessly as they chirp (孜孜) with all their might.

7. 青蟲不易捕 ,
Fresh worms were not easy to catch as prey,

8. 黃口無飽期。
And the young mouths (黃口) were not satiated any day.

9. 嘴爪雖欲敝，
Beaks and talons were about to be tattered (敝),

10. 心力不知疲。
Yet the minds and bodies knew no tired.

11. 須臾十來往，
In an instant, making ten flights to and fro,

12. 猶恐巢中飢。
Still fearing starvation in the nest might take hold.

13. 辛勤三十日，
Working hard for thirty days,

14. 母瘦雛漸肥。
The mother became thin while the chicks gradually gained more weight.

15. 喃喃教言語，
Murmuring to teach them how to speak,

16. 一一刷毛衣。
Brushing every one of them to keep their feathery coats neat.

17. 一旦羽翼長，
Once their wings had grown and could expand,

18. 引上庭樹枝。
It was time to lead them to a straight tree branch.

19. 舉翅不回顧，
The youngsters all spread their wings without looking back,

20. 隨風四散飛。
Taking flight and dispersing with the wind, leaving no track.

21. 雌雄空中鳴，
She and he cried out for the little ones in midair,

22. 聲盡呼不歸。
Not even one returned as their voices were exhausted in despair.

23. 卻入空巢裏，
Nonetheless, the couple retired into their empty nest,

24. 啁啾終夜悲。
Tweeting all night and feeling sad.

25. 燕燕爾勿悲，
O dear swallows, you two should not have been so sad,

26. 爾當反自思。
You should have reflected upon yourselves instead.

27. 思爾為雛日，
The days when you were little chick toddlers,

28. 高飛背母時。
You, too, took flight and turned your backs on your mothers.

29. 當時父母念，
Back then, your parents' minds of sorrow,

30. 今日爾應知！
This day, you shall fully know!

(translated by KS Vincent Poon, Feb 2018, revised Oct 2023)

Remarks

A Poem for the Swallows (《燕詩》/《燕詩示劉叟》) was composed by the renowned poet Bai Juyi (白居易, 772-846AD) of the Tang Dynasty[1]. This work is well-known in traditional Chinese society, for it succinctly illustrates the importance of abiding by Confucian filial piety (孝). According to literature, Bai wrote this poem to depict his sad elderly friend, Lau, whose son had taken off and never returned [2]:

> 叟有愛子，背叟逃去，叟甚悲念之。叟少年時，亦嘗如是。故作《燕詩》以諭之矣。
>
> An elderly man had a dear son. The son turned his back on the elderly man and fled the elderly man without a trace. The elderly depressed man missed him dearly. Yet, when the elderly man was young, he likewise did the same to his parents. *A Poem for the Swallows* was thus composed to let the elderly man understand his frustration.
>
> (translated by KS Vincent Poon, Sept 2023)

Footnotes

(1). 朱金城,《白居易集箋校》. Shanghai: 上海古籍出版社, 1988, p.53.

(2). Ibid..

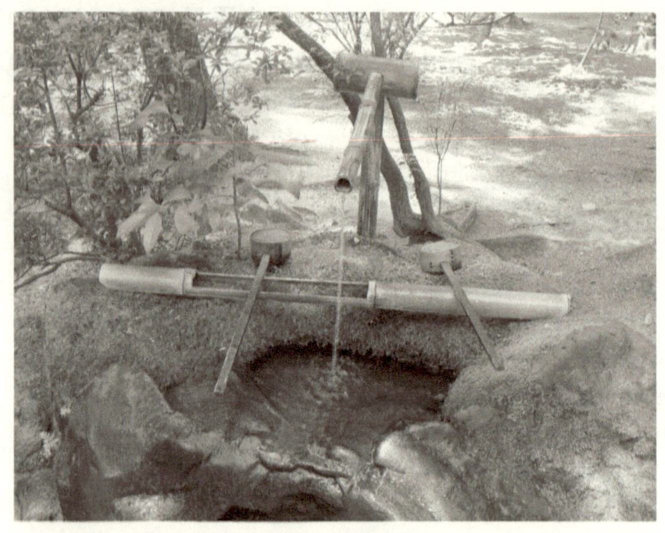

As One Drinks the Water, Always Remember Its Origin
飲水思源
Toshodai-ji Temple
唐招提寺
Nara Japan
Photographed by KS Vincent Poon
2018

Liu Yuxi
Lyrics to the Folk Song
The Bamboo Branches (VII)

劉禹錫
《竹枝詞》(其七)

Calligraphy

Calligrapher (書者): KS Vincent Poon (潘君尚)

Content (內容): *Lyrics to the Folk Song The Bamboo Branches (VII),* a lyrical poem by Liu Yuxi (劉禹錫《竹枝詞》, 其七)

Style (字體): Cursive Script (草書)

Caption (款識): 劉禹錫竹枝詞潘君尚 (Liu Yuxi *Lyrics to the Folk Song The Bamboo Branches,* Kwan Sheung Vincent Poon)

Seal Inscription (鈐印): 潘 (白文) (Poon, white character)

Medium (材料): Ink on Xuan paper (紙墨水本)

Size (尺寸): 94 X 42cm

Year (年份): 2023

瞿塘嘈嘈十二滩，
此中道路古来难。
长恨人心不如水，
等闲平地起波澜。

刘禹锡竹枝词 洋天书

Translation

劉禹錫《竹枝詞》(其七)
Liu Yuxi, *Lyrics to the Folk Song The Bamboo Branches (VII)*

1. 瞿塘嘈嘈十二灘 ,
Qutang (瞿塘)[1] roars (嘈嘈) with a dozen (十二)[2] rapids (灘)[3] that flow fast,

2. 此中道路古來難。
Passages therein have always been difficult to pass.

3. 長恨人心不如水 ,
Long have I resented the human mind is not like that of water,

4. 等閒平地起波瀾。
Suddenly and without reason (等閒平地)[4], it creates all sorts of billows in short order.

(translated by KS Vincent Poon, April 2023)

Remarks

(I)

This lyrical poem is the work of Liu Yuxi (劉禹錫, 772-842 AD)[5] of the Tang Dynasty. It was composed in 822 AD[6] when Liu was demoted from the capital to become the Governor of Kuizhou (夔州刺史)[7].

(II)

Qutang (瞿塘) is renowned for its many turbulent rapids, especially during spring when the frost melts to generate torrents of water. As Li Bai (李白, 701-762 AD) once wrote in his *Jingzhou Song* (《荊州歌》):

瞿塘五月誰敢過?[8]
Who dares to cross Qutang during May?
(translated by KS Vincent Poon)

Yet, even with its fearsome ferocity, Qutang is still much more predictable than humans.

Footnotes

(1). "瞿塘" refers to the "Qutang Gorge (瞿塘峽)", which resided in the province of Kuizhou (夔州). See 《漢語大詞典》. Shanghai: 上海辭書出版社, 2008, p.10863.

(2). "十二" refers to the twelve treacherous rapids in the Qutang Gorge. See 梁守中 《劉禹錫詩文選譯》. Chengdu: 巴蜀書社, 1990, p.40. However, some contend that it merely means "many". See 俞平伯《唐詩鑒賞辭典》. Shanghai: 上海辭書出版社, 2004, p.842.

(3). "灘" here is "the appearance of waters that flow rapidly (水奔流貌)". See 《康熙字典》. Shanghai: 上海書店, 1985, p.731.

(4). "等閒" here means "without reason (無端)", as in 歐陽修 《南歌子•鳳髻金泥帶》："等閒妨了繡功夫, 笑問雙鴛鴦字, 怎生書?" See 《漢語大詞典》. Shanghai: 上海辭書出版社, 2008, p.12297. "平地" here means "suddenly (忽然的)", as in 曹靜照 《西江月•午倦懨懨欲睡》："鶯兒對對話花梢, 平地把人驚覺." See 《漢語大詞典》. Shanghai: 上海辭書出版社, 2008, p.2669. Also, 《眉廬叢話》, Vol.8.

(5). 《全唐詩》 compiled by 曹寅, Vol. 28. 欽定四庫全書薈要集部全唐詩, 康熙四十六年版, p.2.

(6). 梁守中, 《劉禹錫詩文選譯》. Chengdu: 巴蜀書社, 1990, p.36.

(7). 歐陽修, 《新唐書》Vol. 93, 劉禹錫傳. Beijing: 中華書局, 1975, pp.5128-5129.

(8). 《全唐詩》 compiled by 曹寅, Vol. 163, as in footnote (5), p.5.

A Phrase From *Platform Sutra*

《六祖壇經》句

Calligraphy

Calligrapher (書者): KS Vincent Poon (潘君尚)

Content (內容):　A Phrase From *Platform Sutra* (《六祖壇經》句)

Style (字體): Standard Script (楷書)

Caption (款識): 禪宗六祖壇經句壬寅初春潘君尚書於尚尚齋 (A Zen Buddhist Phrase from *Platform Sutra*, during early spring of the year Renyin, Kwan Sheung Vincent Poon scribed at The Senseis)

Seal Inscription (鈐印): 君尚 (朱文) (Kwan Sheung Vincent, red characters), 潘氏 (白文) (The Surname of Poon, white characters)

Medium (材料): Ink on Xuan paper (紙墨水本)

Size (尺寸): 70 X 31cm

Year (年份): 2022

壹燈能除千年暗
一智能滅萬年愚

禪宗六祖壇經句壬寅初春潘君尚書於尚尚齋

Translation

《六祖壇經》句
A Phrase From *Platform Sutra*

1. 一燈能除千年暗,
A single light can wipe out ten centuries of darkness,

2. 一智能滅萬年愚。
A single Wisdom can eradicate ten millennia of foolishness.

(translated by KS Vincent Poon, April 2022)

Remarks

(I)

These words were spoken by the venerable Zen-Buddhist Sixth Patriarch Huineng (禪宗六祖惠能) and documented in the canonical *Platform Sutra* (《 六祖壇經 》).

(II)

"Wisdom (智, 般若, Prajñā)", according to Huineng, is inherent[1] and manifested when one recognizes the intrinsic "non-duality (不二/無二)" of all things[2]. "Non-duality" means the two sides of any contrasting pair (like "good" vs "evil", "tall" vs "short", "light" vs "dark", etc.) actually do not exist, and so it is foolish to favour one side over the other[3,4]. Huineng further elaborated that all such contrasting pairs are mere tools to facilitate human understanding. Ultimately, these tools should be let go once enlightened[5].

Footnotes

(1). 六祖云: "菩提般若之智, 世人本自有之." See 宗寶 《六祖大師法寶壇經》. Taipei: Chinese Buddhist Electronic Text Association (中華電子佛典協會, CBETA).

(2). 佛言: "善根有二: 一者常, 二者無常, 佛性非常非無常, 是故不斷, 名為不二. 一者善, 二者不善, 佛性非善非不善, 是名不二. 蘊之與界, 凡夫見二, 智者了達其性無二, 無二之性即是佛性." Ibid..

(3). 六祖云: "善惡雖殊, 本性無二, 無二之性, 名為實性. 於實性中, 不染善惡, 此名圓滿報身佛." Ibid..

(4). 六祖云: "明與無明, 凡夫見二; 智者了達 , 其性無二. 無二之性, 即是實性. 實性者, 處凡愚而不減, 在賢聖而不增, 住煩惱而不亂, 居禪定而不寂. 不斷不常, 不來不去, 不在中間及其內外, 不生不滅, 性相如如, 常住不遷, 名之曰道." Ibid..

(5). 六祖云: "天與地對, 日與月對, 明與暗對...長與短對, 邪與正對, 癡與慧對, 愚與智對...此三十六對法, 若解用即道, 貫一切經法, 出入即離兩邊. 自性動用, 共人言語, 外於相離相, 內於空離空. 若全著相, 即長邪見; 若全執空, 即長無明." Ibid..

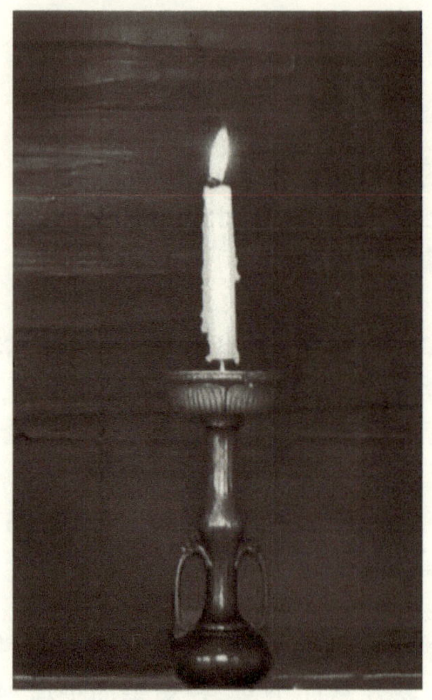

A Candle

一燈

Yakushi-ji Temple

薬師寺

Nara Japan

Photographed by KS Vincent Poon

2018

Pang Yun
A Zen Phrase

龐蘊
禪句

Calligraphy

Calligrapher (書者): KS Vincent Poon (潘君尚)

Content (內容): A Zen Phrase by Pang Yun (龐蘊禪句)

Style (字體): Cursive Script (草書)

Caption (款識): 龐蘊句君尚 (A Zen phrase by Pang Yun, Kwan Sheung Vincent)

Seal Inscription (鈐印): 尚尚齋 (朱文) (The Senseis, red characters), 潘 (白文) (Poon, white character)

Medium (材料): Ink on Xuan paper (紙墨水本)

Size (尺寸): 80 X 35cm

Year (年份): 2022

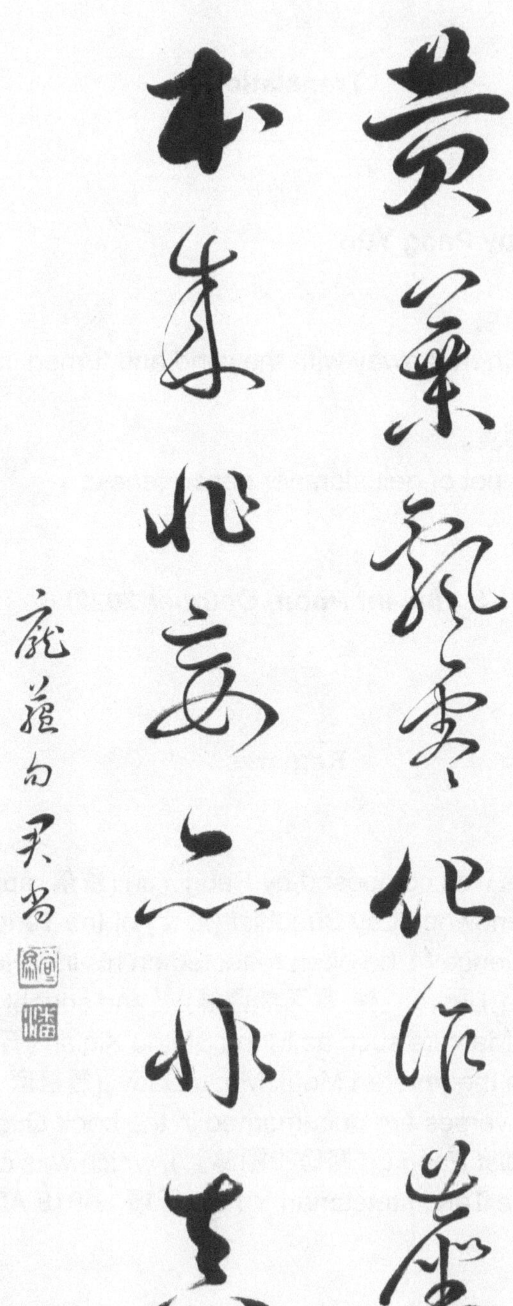

Translation

龐蘊禪句
A Zen Phrase by Pang Yun

1. 黃葉飄零化作塵,
A yellow leaf withered away with the wind and turned into dust,

2. 本來非妄亦非真。
Fundamentally, not of delusion nor concreteness.

(translated by KS Vincent Poon, October 2022)

Remarks

This Zen phrase was composed by Pang Yun (龐蘊, approx. 740-808 AD)[1], a renowned Lay Buddhist (居士) of the Tang Dynasty. Despite his affluence[2], he often reflected on his life. He befriended Monk Danxia Tianran (丹霞天然禪師)[3] and sought tutelage from other Zen Masters such as Monk Shitou Xiqian (石頭希遷禪師)[4] as well as the revered Monk Mazu Daoyi (馬祖道一禪師)[5]. His poems and verses are documented in the book *Quotations from Lay Buddhist Pang* (《龐居士語錄》), which was compiled by the venerable Tang statesman Yu Di (于頔, ?-818 AD)[6].

Footnotes

(1).《龐居士語錄》compiled by 于頔 , Vol.3. Taipei: Chinese Buddhist Electronic Text Association (中華電子佛典協會, CBETA).

(2). "(龐蘊)嘗以舡載家珍數萬". See 《釋氏通鑑》 compiled by 本覺, Vol. 9. CBETA, ibid..

(3).《釋氏稽古略》 compiled by 覺岸, Vol. 9. CBETA, ibid..

(4). 超永, 《五燈全書》 Vol. 6. CBETA, ibid..

(5). Ibid..

(6). As in footnote (1).

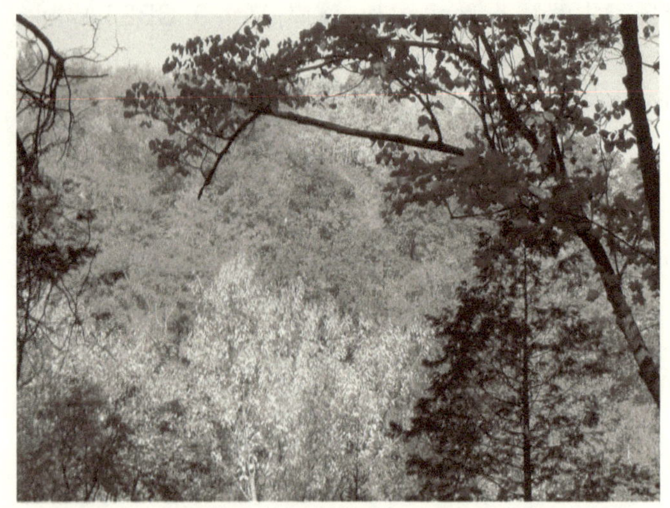

The Autumn Yellow Leaves

秋黃葉

Belfountain Canada

Photographed by KS Vincent Poon

2004

Li Qingzhao
A Quatrain Written in a Summer

李清照
《夏日絕句》

Calligraphy

Calligrapher (書者): KS Vincent Poon (潘君尚)

Content (內容): *A Quatrain Written in a Summer,* a poem by Li Qingzhao (李清照《夏日絕句》)

Style (字體): Clerical Script (隸書)

Caption (款識): 李清照夏日絕句潘君尚(Li Qingzhao *A Quatrain Written in a Summer,* Kwan Sheung Vincent Poon)

Seal Inscription (鈐印): 潘 (朱文) (Poon, red character), 君尚 (白文) (Kwan Sheung Vincent, white characters)

Medium (材料): Ink on Xuan paper (紙墨水本)

Size (尺寸): 72 X 38cm

Year (年份): 2023

生當作人傑，死亦為鬼雄。至今思項羽，不肯過江東。

李清照　夏日絶句　潘君尚

Translation

李清照《夏日絕句》
Li Qingzhao, *A Quatrain Written in a Summer*

1. 生當作人傑,
Live to be a person with gallant valour,

2. 死亦爲鬼雄。
Die to become a ghost with a heroic aura.

3. 至今思項羽,
Even now, we all remember Xiang Yu[1], the conqueror,

4. 不肯過江東。
For he willed not to retreat East by crossing the Wu River[2].

(translated by KS Vincent Poon, March 2023)

Remarks

(I)

This poem was composed by Li Qingzhao (李清照, 1084 – 1151 AD) of the Song Dynasty. It was written in 1129 AD[3] when she followed her husband, Zhao Mingcheng (趙明誠, 1081-1129 AD), to flee Jiankang (建康, now Nanjing, 南京) from the northern invading Jurchens (女真)[4]. This poem expresses her anguish in having a husband who chose not to stand his ground honorably to fight against the invaders.

(II)

Li was born into an aristocratic family. Her father, Li Gefei (李格非, 1045-1105 AD) was a renowned literati[5] and a revered government official[6]. Her mother was also adept at writing[7]. At a very young age, Li married Zhao Mingcheng, who was a scholar[8] and the son of senior statesman Zhao Tingzhi (趙挺之, 1040-1107 AD)[9]. After marriage, Li helped Zhao Mingcheng complete his masterpiece *Catalogue of Bronze and Stone Inscriptions* (《金石錄》) [10].

(III)

Li is often regarded as the greatest female poet in Chinese history[11]. Contemporary scholar Zheng Zhenduo (鄭振鐸, 1898-1958 AD) held Li's literary style was so unique that it "had never been achieved before and will never be equalled in the future (前無古人, 後無來者)"[12]. Regrettably, most of her writings were lost during the Jurchen invasion[13].

Footnotes

(1). Xiang Yu (項羽, 232-202BC) was the conqueror who overthrew the Qin Dynasty. He later lost decisively to Liu Bang (劉邦, 256-195 BC) in the Battle of Gaixia (垓下之戰), refused to retreat with shame, and eventually committed suicide at the Wu River (烏江). See 司馬遷 《史記》 Vol. 7, 項羽本紀. Hong Kong: 廣智書局, publication year unknown, p.26.

(2). Many interpret "江東" as Jiandong, the region southeast of the Yangtze River (長江), the home of Xiang Yu. However, judging from the documentation of the Battle of Gaixia (垓下之戰) in 《史記》 and the usage of "cross (過)", "江" in the poem undoubtedly refers to "Wu River (烏江)".

(3). 徐培均, 《李清照集箋注》. Shanghai: 上海古籍出版社, 2002, p.238.

(4). 趙明誠,《金石錄》, Li Qingzhao's epilogue 《金石錄後序》. 欽定四庫全書 史部, 乾隆四十一年版, pp.1-6.

(5). 鄭振鐸, 《中國文學史》. Shanghai: Shanghai Commerical Press, 1932, p.505.

(6). 脫脫 ,《宋史》Vol. 444, 李格非傳. Taipei: 藝文印書館, 乾隆武英殿版, Book 7, pp.5390-5391.

(7). 鄭振鐸, as in footnote (5), p.506.

(8). Ibid..

(9). 《宋史》, as in footnote (6), p.5391.

(10). 李清照, as in footnote (4).

(11). 鄭振鐸, as in footnote (5).

(12). Ibid..

(13). Ibid..

A Phrase From
Analects – Xue Er

《論語·學而》句

Calligraphy

Calligrapher (書者): KS Vincent Poon (潘君尚)

Content (內容): A Phrase From *Analects - Xue Er* (《論語•學而》句)

Style (字體): Cursive Script (草書)

Caption (款識): 論語學而己亥潘君尚 (*The Analects of Confucius - Xue Er.* Year of the Jihai, Kwan Sheung Vincent Poon)

Seal Inscription (鈐印): 君尚 (朱文) (Kwan Sheung Vincent, red characters), 潘 (白文) (Poon, white character)

Medium (材料): Ink on Xuan paper (紙墨水本)

Size (尺寸): 67 X 34cm

Year (年份): 2019

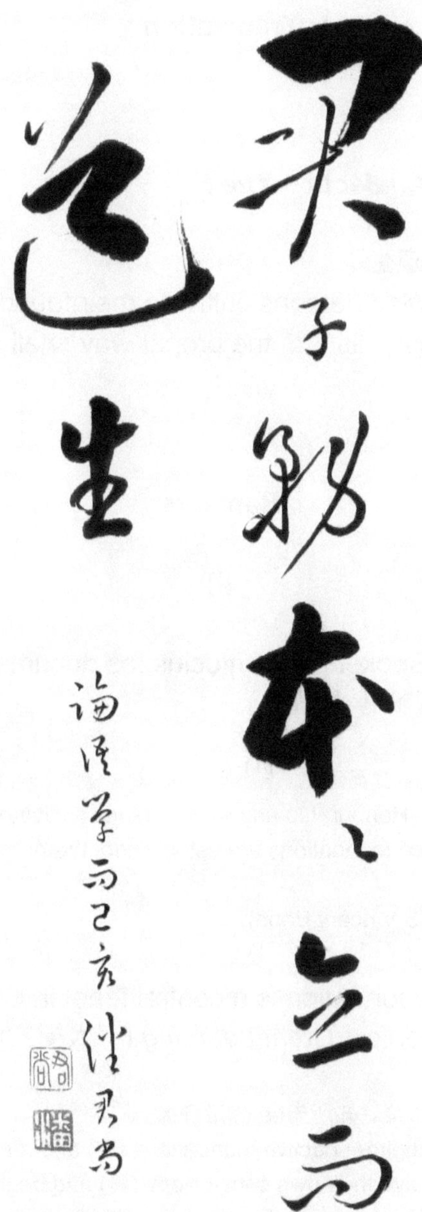

君子務本　本立而道生
論語學而　己亥　書

Translation

《論語•學而》句
A Phrase From *Analects – Xue Er*

君子務本, 本立而道生 。
Honourable and wise persons cultivate their foundations; once foundations are established, the proper way shall emerge.

Remarks

(I)

This phrase was spoken by Confucius, as documented in *Analects - Xue Er* (《論語•學而》):

子曰: 君子務本, 本立而道生。[1]
Confucius said, "Honourable and wise persons cultivate their foundations; once foundations are established, the proper way shall emerge."
(translated by KS Vincent Poon)

Prioritizing one's foundation is a central tenet in Confucian philosophy. The canonical *Great Learning* (《大學》) dictates:

物有本末, 事有終始。知所先後, 則近道矣。[2]
All things have their respective foundations (本) and ramifications (末); all affairs have their own conclusions (終) and beginnings (始). If one knows which comes before and which comes after, then one

shall not be far from The Fundamental Way (道) of the *Great Learning*.

(translated by KS Vincent Poon)

(II)

For rulers, cultivating good foundations is not only beneficial for themselves but also for their governance, according to renowned Confucian scholar Liu Xiang (劉向, 77-6 BC):

孔子曰:「君子務本, 本立而道生。」 夫本不正者末必倚, 始不盛者終必衰 … 有正春者無亂秋, 有正君者無危國…是故君子貴建本而重立始。(3)

Confucius said, "Honourable and wise persons cultivate their foundations; once foundations are established, the proper way shall emerge." Alas, an improper foundation leads to ramifications that will go astray, and an impoverished beginning will conclude in a downfall … A proper Spring does not give rise to a chaotic Autumn, and a proper ruler does not give rise to a nation in peril…Thus, honourable and wise persons hold building their foundations in high regard and pay great attention when establishing a beginning.

(translated by KS Vincent Poon)

Indeed, good foundations (本) beget good ramifications (末). In parallel to this, Mengzi (孟子, 372-289 BC) contended only good rulers are awarded loyal subordinates:

君之視臣如手足, 則臣視君如腹心; 君之視臣如犬馬, 則臣視君如國人; 君之視臣如土芥, 則臣視君如寇讎。(4)

If rulers regard their subordinates as their own hands and feet, then their subordinates shall regard their rulers as their own abdomens and hearts; if rulers regard their subordinates as dogs and horses, then their subordinates shall regard their rulers as ordinary laymen; if rulers regard their subordinates as dirt and grass, then their subordinates shall regard their rulers as sworn enemies.

(translated by KS Vincent Poon)

(III)

It is then clear that a ruler must first become fit to be a ruler **before** a subordinate becomes fit to be a subordinate. Hence, Confucian philosopher Dong Zhongshu (董仲舒, 179-104 BC) once wrote:

父不父則子不子, 君不君則臣不臣耳。 [5]
If the father is unfit to be a father, then the son shall be unfit to be a son; if the ruler is unfit to be a ruler, then the subordinate shall be unfit to be a subordinate.
(translated by KS Vincent Poon)

Confucian philosophy originally never endorses "blind loyalty (愚忠)" nor asks one to "blindly pay respect to their parents (愚孝)". Rulers and parents must do their part first.

As defined by Xu Shen (許慎, 58-148 AD) in *Shuowen Jiezi* (《說文解字》), "The character 'Benevolence (仁)' is derived from the characters 'Person and Two (从人二)' "[6]. Benevolence is always bilateral, never unilateral.

Footnotes

(1) 《論語•學而》. See 朱熹,《四書集註》. Hong Kong: 太平書局, 1968 , p.1.

(2) KS Vincent Poon, *Calligraphy Meets Philosophy Talk 1*. Toronto: The Senseis, 2022, p.24.

(3) 劉向,《說苑》Vol.3, 建本. 欽定四庫全書子部, 乾隆四十六年版, p.1.

(4) 《孟子•離婁下》. See 朱熹,《四書集註》. Hong Kong: 太平書局 , 1968, pp.111-112.

(5) 董仲舒,《春秋繁露》 Vol.1, 玉杯. 欽定四庫全書經部, 乾隆四十二年版, p.9.

(6) 段玉裁,《說文解字注》. Taipei: 藝文印書館, 1966, p.369.

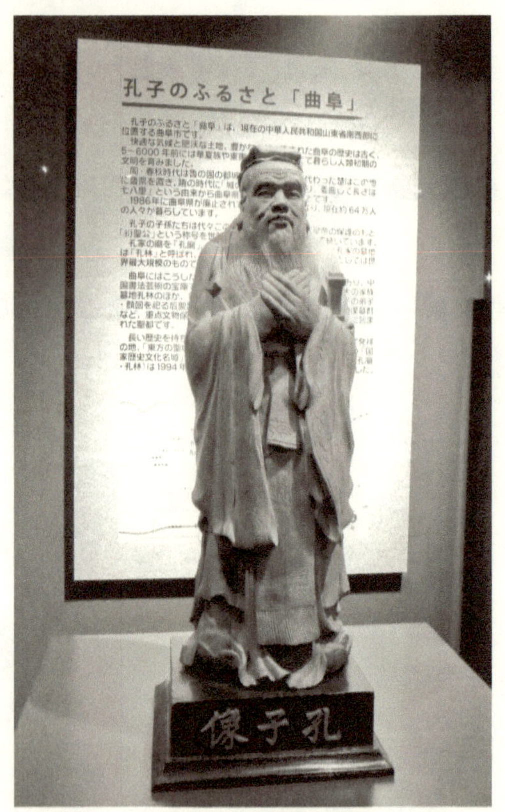

A Confucius Statue
孔子像
Nagasaki Koshibyo Confucius Shrine
長崎孔子廟
Nagasaki Japan
Photographed by KS Vincent Poon
2023

Sima Guang
The Family Precepts of Sima Guang

司馬光
《司馬溫公家訓》

Calligraphy

Calligrapher (書者): KS Vincent Poon (潘君尚)

Content (內容): *The Family Precepts of Sima Guang* by Sima Guang (司馬光《司馬溫公家訓》)

Style (字體): Standard Script (楷書)

Caption (款識): 司馬温公家訓二千二十四年潘君尚書 (*The Family Precepts of Sima Guang*, the year two-thousand twenty-four, scribed by Kwan Sheung Vincent Poon)

Seal Inscription (鈐印): 君尚 (朱文) (Kwan Sheung Vincent, red characters), 潘氏 (白文) (The Surname of Poon, white characters)

Medium (材料): Ink on Xuan paper (紙墨水本)

Size (尺寸): 66 X 35cm

Year (年份): 2024

積金以遺子孫未必守積書以遺子孫未必讀不如積陰德於冥冥之間為子孫長久之計此先賢之格言乃後人之龜鑑

司馬溫公家訓　二千廿四年潘君尚書

Translation

司馬光 《司馬溫公家訓》
Sima Guang, *The Family Precepts of Sima Guang*

1. 積金以遺子孫，子孫未必守。
Amass wealth for your descendants, but your descendants may not be able to sustain it.

2. 積書以遺子孫，子孫未必讀。
Amass books for your descendants, but your descendants may not read them.

3. 不如積陰德於冥冥之間，為子孫長久之計。
It is thus better to amass "tacit deeds of grace (陰德)"[1] within this governed Cosmos (冥冥)[2], for this is the lasting way to benefit your descendants.

4. 此先賢之格言，乃後人之龜鑑。
Such is an adage passed on by the ancient sages and a mirror with which future generations can reflect themselves (龜鑑)[3].

(translated by KS Vincent Poon, January 2024)

Remarks

(I)

Sima Guang (司馬光, 1019-1086 AD) is often regarded as one of the greatest historians in Chinese history. His most influential work, *Zizhi Tongjian* (《資治通鑑》), details the history of ancient China between BC 403 and AD 958[4]. As a government official, Sima Guang was renowned for his principled opposition to Wang Anshan's reforms (王安石變法) during the reign of Emperor Shenzong (宋神宗, 1048-1085) of the Song Dynasty[5]. Upon his death, he was bestowed the title "Duke of Weng (溫國公)" by Emperor Zhezong (宋哲宗, 1077-1100)[6].

(II)

The term "tacit deeds of grace (陰德)" can be found as early as the 1st century BC in the book *Shuo Yuan* (《說苑》) by Liu Huang (劉向, 77-6 BC), a Confucian:

夫有陰德者必有陽報。[7]
Alas, those who carry out tacit deeds of grace shall be awarded explicit and tangible rewards in this world.
(translated by KS Vincent Poon)

This idea can be regarded as an extension of a concept in the *Book of Documents* (《尚書》), the oldest book in Chinese history:

作善降之百祥，作不善降之百殃。 [8]
Those who do good deeds shall be granted many good fortunes,
while those who do misdeeds shall be granted many misfortunes.
(translated by KS Vincent Poon)

(III)

Good fortunes delivered by "tacit deeds of grace (陰德)" can even
reach one's descendants, according to some:

A. 夏侯勝曰:「有陰德者必饗其樂以及其子孫。」 [9]
Xiahou Sheng once said, "Those who carry out tacit deeds of grace
will enjoy the resulting happiness, and so will their descendants."
(translated by KS Vincent Poon)

B. 于公曰:「我治獄多陰德, 未嘗有所冤, 子孫必有興者。」 [10]
Elder Yu once said, "I conducted many tacit deeds of grace as I
administrated the prison, and there was never injustice. My descendants will thus bear prosperous ones."
(translated by KS Vincent Poon)

In the second instance above, Elder Yu's (于公, ?-? BC) tacit
deeds of grace allowed his son, Yu Dingguo (于定國, ?-40BC), to
learn his father's way of justice and compassion[11]. Yu Dinggou
eventually became the Chancellor (丞相) of the Han Dynasty[12].

Footnotes

(1). "陰德" here means "tacit deeds of grace for others (暗中做的
有德於人的事)", as in *Huainanzi - In the World of Man* (《淮南子·
人間訓》): "有陰德者必有陽報, 有陰行者必有昭名." See 《漢語大詞典》. Shanghai: 上海辭書出版社, 2008, p.1035.

(2). "冥冥" here means "the Cosmos governed by a higher power which oversees the human realm (主宰人世禍福的神靈世界)", as in 沈作喆's《寓簡》: "豈人之禍福吉凶自有定數存於冥冥之中, 雖聖與智不可得而逃耶?" See 《漢語大詞典》. Shanghai: 上海辭書出版社, 2008, p.452.

(3). "龜" here refers to "tortoiseshell (龜甲) ", which was used in ancient China "to tell fortune and misfortune (占卜吉凶)". "鑑" refers to "a mirror (鏡子)" that can "reflect whether something is beautiful or not (照見美醜)". "龜鑑" is thus a metaphor for "admonition and self-reflection (警戒和反省)", as in *History of Song – Biography of Bao Zheng* (《宋史•包拯傳》): "又列上唐魏鄭公三疏, 願置之坐右, 以為龜鑑." See 《漢語大詞典》. Shanghai: 上海辭書出版社, 2008, p.1513.

(4). 司馬光,《資治通鑑》, 胡三省注, 新校提要. Hong Kong: 世界書局, 1970, p.1.

(5). 脫脫,《宋史》Vol.336, 司馬光傳. Taipei: 藝文印書館, 乾隆武英殿版, pp.4245-4246.

(6). Ibid., p.4248.

(7). 劉向,《說苑》Vol.5, 貴德. 欽定四庫全書子部, 乾隆四十六年版, p.2b.

(8). 孔安國,《尚書孔傳》商書伊訓. Taipei: 新興書局, 1964, p.024.

(9). 劉向,《說苑》Vol.6, 復恩. As in footnote (7), pp.5a-5b.

(10). 班固,《漢書》Vol.71, 于定國傳. 香港: 中華書局, 1970, p.3046.

(11). Ibid., p.3042.

(12). Ibid., p.3043.

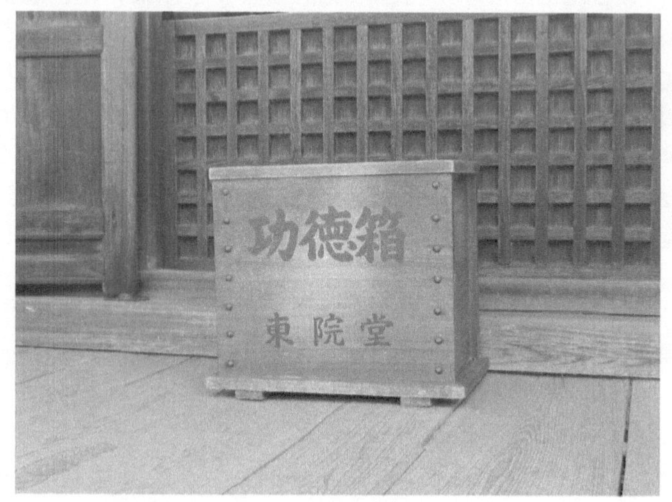

An Offering Box for Amassing One's Merit
功德箱
Toindo, Yakushi-ji Temple
東院堂, 藥師寺
Nara Japan
Photographed by KS Vincent Poon
2018

A Phrase From
A Narrative on Calligraphy

《書譜》句

Calligraphy

Calligrapher (書者): KS Vincent Poon (潘君尚)

Content (內容): A Phrase From *A Narrative on Calligraphy* (《書譜》句)

Style (字體): Clerical Script (隸書)

Caption (款識): 君尚 (Kwan Sheung Vincent)

Seal Inscription (鈐印): 君尚 (朱文) (Kwan Sheung Vincent, red characters), 潘氏 (白文) (The Surname of Poon, white characters)

Medium (材料): Ink on Xuan paper (紙墨水本)

Size (尺寸): 40 X 23cm

Year (年份): 2023

俯習寸陰
尺尚

Translation

《書譜》句
A Phrase From *A Narrative on Calligraphy*

俛習寸陰 。
Devote every moment to learning and practising.
(translated by KS Vincent Poon, January 2024)

Remarks

(I)

This phrase was drafted by Sun Guoting (孫過庭, 648-703 AD) in his *A Narrative on Calligraphy* (《書譜》)[1], an authoritative monograph on Chinese calligraphy. He used this expression to encourage calligraphers to learn and practise the art tirelessly to reach the highest level of excellence[2].

(II)

Confucius enshrined devotion to learning, for it reveals wisdom to the mind:

好學近乎知。 [3]
Those who love learning are approaching close to wisdom.
(translated by KS Vincent Poon)

Confucius further contended persistent learning and practising can lead to joy and satisfaction:

學而時習之，不亦說乎？[4]
To learn and to constantly practise one's learning, is it not delightful?
(translated by KS Vincent Poon)

Thus, Confucius once said, "I never grow tired of learning (我學不厭)."[5]

Footnotes

(1). KS Vincent Poon & Kwok Kin Poon, *A Narrative on Calligraphy by Sun Guoting Revised and Enhanced Edition*. Toronto: The Senseis, 2019, p.18.

(2). Ibid., pp.15-19.

(3). 《中庸》. See 朱熹,《四書集註》. Hong Kong: 太平書局, 1968 , p.16.

(4). 《論語•學而》. Ibid., p.1.

(5). 《孟子•公孫丑上》. Ibid., p.41.

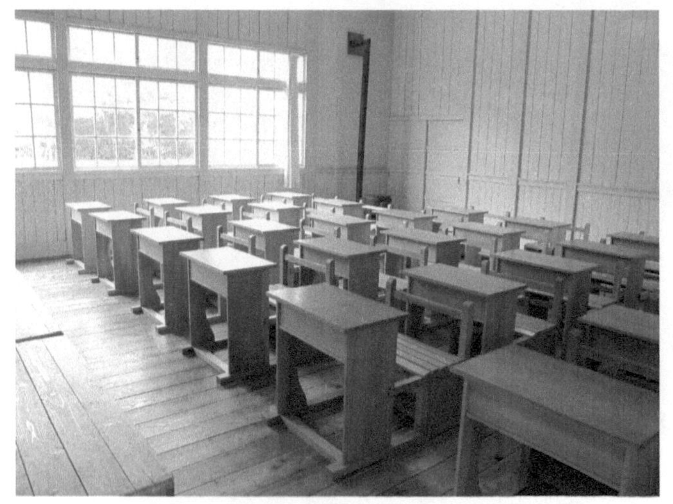

A Classroom
課室
Historical Village of Hokkaido
北海道開拓の村
Sapporo Japan
Photographed by KS Vincent Poon
2010

A Phrase From
New Book of Tang –
Comments on the Biography of
Yan Zhenqing

《新唐書·顏真卿傳贊》句

Calligraphy

Calligrapher (書者): KS Vincent Poon (潘君尚)

Content (內容):　A Phrase From *New Book of Tang – Comments on the Biography of Yan Zhenqing* (《新唐書•顏真卿傳贊》句)

Style (字體): Clerical Script (隸書)

Caption (款識): 君尚 (Kwan Sheung Vincent)

Seal Inscription (鈐印): 潘氏 (白文) (The Surname of Poon, white characters)

Medium (材料): Ink on Xuan paper (紙墨水本)

Size (尺寸):　25 X 71cm

Year (年份): 2023

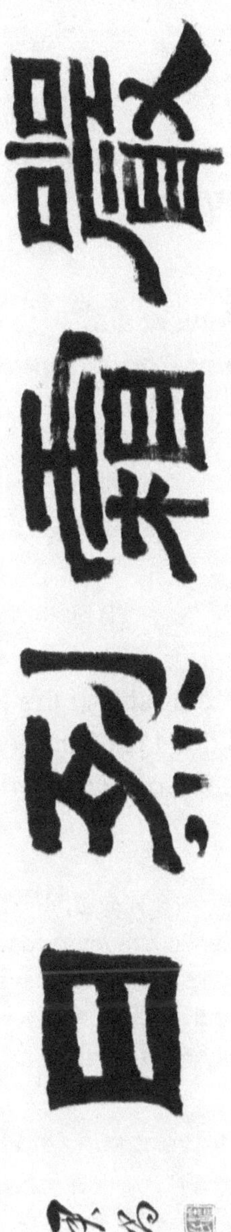

Translation

《新唐書•顏真卿傳贊》句
A Phrase From *New Book of Tang – Comments on the Biography of Yan Zhenqing*

嚴霜烈日。
The fierce frost and the fervent sun.
(translated by KS Vincent Poon, January 2024)

Remarks

(I)

The expression "The fierce frost and the fervent sun (嚴霜烈日)" can be found as early as the 11th Century in *New Book of Tang – Comments on the Biography of Yan Zhenqing* (《新唐書•顏真卿傳贊》):

其英烈言言，如嚴霜烈日，可畏而仰哉![1]
His (Yan Zhenqing's) ardent courageousness (英烈)[2] and noble solemnity (言言)[3] were like the fierce frost and the fervent sun, and he is to be revered (畏) and venerated (仰), indeed!
(translated by KS Vincent Poon)

"The fierce frost and the fervent sun (嚴霜烈日)" is parallel to the Japanese proverb "秋霜烈日", which today's Japanese prosecutors use as their creed and refine their temperaments to uphold "Fīat Jūstitia Ruat Cælum (Let Justice Be Done though the Heavens Fall)".

(II)

Yan Zhenqing (顏真卿, AD 709-785) was a venerable Tang Dynasty commander who helped quell the rebellious An Lushan (安祿山, 703-757AD)[4]. As a young man, he was already an avid learner and practitioner of Confucian values and was bestowed the title of "Jinshi (進士)" at age 25[5]. Within the bureaucracy, he was well-known for his outspokenness, which led him to be demoted and re-promoted several times[6]. In his final days, Yan showed his noble and unrelenting temperament by refusing to surrender to the treacherous Li Xilie (李希烈, ?-786AD) in the face of execution[7]. In addition to his remarkable bureaucratic career, Yan was also widely recognized as a distinguished calligrapher who penned many classical masterpieces, including *A Poem on General Pei* (《裴將軍詩》)[8].

Footnotes

(1). 歐陽修,《新唐書》Vol.153, 顏真卿傳. Beijing: 中華書局, 1975, p.4861.

(2). "英烈" here means "ardent and courageous (勇敢而有氣節)", as in 劉大櫆《鄉飲賓金君傳》: "長洪字師林, 少從塾師讀書, 聞先生述古孝義長者英烈之事, 竊聽常罔倦." See《漢語大詞典》. Shanghai: 上海辭書出版社, 2008, p.343.

(3). "言言" here means "solemn (威嚴)" , as in 劉禹錫《吏部侍郎奚公神道碑》: "惟唐德宗, 道類漢宣, 責實繩下, 風稜言言." See《漢語大詞典》. Shanghai: 上海辭書出版社, 2008, p.5.

(4). As in footnote (1), p.4854.

(5). 黃本驥,《顏魯公全集》, 顏魯公集行狀. Shanghai: 上海仿古書店, publication year unknown, p.11.

(6). As in footnote (1), pp.4854-4859.

(7). Ibid., p.4860.

(8). KS Vincent Poon & Kwok Kin Poon, *English Translation of Classical Chinese Calligraphy Masterpieces*. Toronto: The Senseis, 2019, p.81-92.

A Phrase From
Book of Rites –
Conveyance of Rites

《禮記·禮運》句

Calligraphy

Calligrapher (書者): KS Vincent Poon (潘君尚)

Content (內容): A Phrase From *Book of Rites - Conveyance of Rites* (《禮記•禮運》句)

Style (字體): Standard Script (楷書)

Caption (款識): 君尚 (Kwan Sheung Vincent)

Seal Inscription (鈐印): 潘 (白文) (Poon, white character)

Medium (材料): Ink on Xuan paper (紙墨水本)

Size (尺寸): 45 X 27cm

Year (年份): 2023

天下為公

君尚

Translation

《禮記•禮運》句
A Phrase From Book of Rites – Conveyance of Rites

天下爲公。
All under heaven belongs to (爲)[1] the public.
(translated by KS Vincent Poon, March 2024)

Remarks

(I)

"All under heaven belongs to the public (天下爲公)" can be found in *Book of Rites - Conveyance of Rites* (《禮記•禮運》):

子曰: 「大道之行也, 天下爲公。」[2]
Confucius said, "When the Great Way prevails, all under heaven belongs to the public."
(translated by KS Vincent Poon)

Confucians use these words to describe the ideal Confucian society wherein no one monopolizes the nation[3]. Successions of power are not hereditary, and everyone can be chosen for public office with no prejudice[4]. Further, since Confucian values prevail, the people trust and love one another, and all can work to the best of their abilities[5]. Confucians describe this utopia as the "Great Unity (大同)"[6].

(II)

Dr Sun Yat Sen (孫逸仙, 1866-1925), Father of the Nation (國父), drew a parallel between his "Principle of Democracy (民權主義)" and the Confucian concept of "All under heaven belongs to the public":

孔子說： 「大道之行也, 天下爲公」, 便是主張民權的大同世界。[7]
Confucius once said, "When the Great Way prevails, all under heaven belongs to the public." This was him advocating for a democratic world of Great Unity.
(translated by KS Vincent Poon)

Indeed, Sun found "All under heaven belongs to the public" so appealing that he eventually wrote a calligraphy of it[8].

Footnotes

(1). "爲" here means "belongs to (歸於/屬於)", as in 《戰國策•秦策一》 : "不用一領甲, 不苦一民, 皆秦之有也. 代、 上黨, 不戰而已爲秦矣. " 姚宏注 : "爲, 猶屬也." See 《剡川姚氏本戰國策》 Vol.3, 秦策一. Shanghai: 鴻寶齋, 1914, p.4.

(2). 鄭玄注, 孔穎達疏, 《禮記注疏》 , 禮運. Shanghai: 中華書局, 1936, p.2.

(3). Ibid..

(4). Ibid., pp.2-3.

(5). Ibid..

(6). Ibid..

(7). 孫中山,《三民主義》, 民權主義第一講. Shanghai: 上海春明書店, 1947, pp.48-49.

(8). 劉正成,《中國書法鑒賞大辭典》. Beijing: 大地出版社, 1989, p.1347.

Sun Yat-sen
The Will of the Father of the Nation

孫逸仙
《國父遺囑》

Calligraphy

Calligrapher (書者): KS Vincent Poon (潘君尚)

Content (內容): *The Will of the Father of the Nation* by Sun Yat-sen (孫逸仙《國父遺囑》)

Style (字體): Standard Script (楷書)

Caption (款識): 國父遺囑癸卯潘君尚書 (*The Will of the Father of the Nation*, year of the Guimao, scribed by Kwan Sheung Vincent Poon)

Seal Inscription (鈐印): 君尚 (朱文) (Kwan Sheung Vincent, red characters), 潘氏 (白文) (The Surname of Poon, white characters)

Medium (材料): Ink on Xuan paper (紙墨水本)

Size (尺寸): 35 X 80cm

Year (年份): 2023

余致力國民革命，凡四十年，其目的在求中國之自由平等。積四十年之經驗，深知欲達到此目的，必須喚起民眾，及聯合世界上以平等待我之民族，共同奮鬥。現在革命尚未成功，凡我同志，務須依照余所著建國方略、建國大綱、三民主義及第一次全國代表大會宣言，繼續努力，以求貫徹。最近主張開國民會議及廢除不平等條約，尤須於最短期間，促其實現。是所至囑！

Translation
(translated by Frank W. Price)[1]

孫逸仙《國父遺囑》
Sun Yat-sen, ***The Will of the Father of the Nation***

1. 余致力國民革命, 凡四十年, 其目的在求中國之自由平等。
For forty years I have devoted myself to the cause of the people's revolution with but one end in view, the elevation of China to a position of freedom and equality among the nations.

2. 積四十年之經驗, 深知欲達到此目的, 必須喚起民眾及聯合世界上以平等待我之民族, 共同奮鬥。
My experiences during these forty years have firmly convinced me that to attain this goal, we must bring about a thorough awakening of our own people and ally ourselves in a common struggle with those peoples of the world who treat us on the basis of equality.

3. 現在革命尚未成功。
The work of the Revolution is not yet done.

4. 凡我同志, 務須依照余所著《建國方略》、《建國大綱》、《三民主義》及《第一次全國代表大會宣言》, 繼續努力, 以求貫徹。
Let all our comrades follow my *Plans for National Reconstruction*, *Fundamentals of National Reconstruction*, *Three Principles of the People*, and the *Manifesto* issued by the First National Convention of our Party, and strive on for their consummation.

5. 最近主張開國民會議及廢除不平等條約, 尤須於最短期間促其實現。是所至囑!

Above all, our recent declarations in favor of the convocation of a National Convention and the abolition of unequal treaties should be carried into effect with the least possible delay. This is my heartfelt charge to you!

Remarks

Dr. Sun Yat-Sen (孫逸仙, 1866-1925) is the greatest revolution- ary in contemporary China and is often revered as the "Father of the Nation (國父)"[2]. He played a critical role in overthrowing the Qing Dynasty and became the first president of the Republic of China (中華民國) in 1912[3]. Sun was also the chief engineer of the "Three People's Principles (三民主義)"[4], which authorita- tive historian Chien Mu (錢穆, 1895-1990) described as "the **only** path to wholly establish the Republic of China (必為中華民國建國完成之<u>惟一</u>路向)"[5].

Sadly, despite Sun's extraordinary achievements, his dream of a just and democratic mainland China never come to fruition.

Footnotes

(1). Price F.W. (translator), *The Principle of Democracy* (孫文 《民權主義》). Taipei: China Cultural Service, 1927, p.(v).

(2). 羅香林,《國父家世源流考》. Publication place unknown, 1946, p.6.

(3). 吳敬恒,《國父孫中山先生年譜》. 中國國民黨中央執行委員會, publication place unknown, 1940, pp.5-49.

(4). 孫中山,《三民主義》. Shanghai: 上海春明書店, 1947.

(5). 錢穆,《國史大綱》. Shanghai: 國立編譯館, p.660.

A Model of *Yi Ying Stele*

臨《乙瑛碑》

Calligraphy

Calligrapher (書者): KS Vincent Poon (潘君尚)

Content (內容): *Yi Ying Stele*, modelled by KS Vincent (潘君尚臨《乙瑛碑》)

Style (字體): Clerical Script (隸書)

Caption (款識): 漢乙瑛碑二千廿三年夏六月潘君尚臨於尚尚齋 (*Yi Ying Stele* of the Han Dynasty, in June during the summer of the year two-thousand twenty-three, modelled by Kwan Sheung Vincent Poon at The Senseis)

Seal Inscription (鈐印): 君尚 (朱文) (Kwan Sheung Vincent, red characters), 潘 (白文) (Poon, white character)

Medium (材料): Ink on Xuan paper (紙墨水本)

Size (尺寸): 66 X 32cm (11 sheets)

Year (年份): 2023

瑛書言諮書崇聖

恭稽首言魯前相

司徒臣雄司空臣

道秋孝經又辟繹
緯天地幽讚神繡
故特立廟慈成族

四時來祠巳即去

廟有禮人掌領請

寔百一人興主守

廟　王　須
春　家　報
秋　錢　謹
饗　給　問
禮　大　大
財　酒　常
出　宜　祠

曹掾馮羊史郭亮
辟行祠先聖師侍
祠者孔子子孫大

宰大祝令各一人
皆備爵大常丞祠
河南帝各一大司農

乾以為漢制作先

如璞言孔子大象

繪米祠里愚以為

世所尊祠如寵子

恭明祀傳于田橄

可許里請魯焉孔

子廟置百石卒一

入掌禮器酒宣如

故事吏雜吏羕愚

戀誠惶誠恐頓首

死罪死罪臣稽首

以聞曰可河季高

元嘉三秊三月廿

亡日王寅奏雄宮

漢乙瑛碑二千廿三年夏六月潘君尚臨於尚尚齋

Remarks

(I)

The *Yi Ying Stele* (《乙瑛碑》) was erected in 153AD during the Eastern Han Dynasty[1] to document the assignment of an officer to oversee a Confucius Shrine (孔廟)[2]. Its calligraphy is often regarded as the best exemplar of the Han clerical script[3], holding qualities of propriety, elegance, and lively variations all at the same time[4]. Thus, some consider it a grand masterpiece that all calligraphers should study[5].

(II)

The text of the *Yi Ying Stele* also serves as an important document in studying Eastern Han history. First, it confirms Wu Xiong (吳雄) was the Imperial Chancellor (司徒) while Zhao Jie (趙戒) was the Imperial Counsellor (司空) around 153AD, as chronicled in *Book of the Later Han* (《後漢書》)[6]. Second, it narrates an individual called Yi Yin (乙瑛) as the Ministerial Governor of Lu (魯相)[7], which is not recorded in *Book of the Later Han*[8]. Third, it provides direct evidence that the Eastern Han highly regarded Confucius and enshrined Confucianism[9].

Footnotes

(1). 劉正成,《中國書法鑒賞大辭典》. Beijing: 大地出版社, 1989, p.95.

(2). 洪适,《隸釋隸續》. Beijing: 中華書局, 1985, pp.18-19.

(3). 方朔云: "(乙瑛碑) 漢隸最可師法者." As in foonote (1).

(4). "(乙瑛碑) 端莊匀實, 體態動人, 輕重變化, 頗多妙趣, 形態飛動遒勁, 表露了渾融瀟逸的韻味". As in foonote (1).

(5). "(乙瑛碑) 屬于東漢刻石的巨制, 亦是今天學習隸書的優良範本". As in footnote (1).

(6). 范曄,《後漢書》Vol.7, 孝桓帝紀. Hong Kong: 中華書局, 1971, pp.297-298; 歐陽修,《集古錄》Vol.2. 欽定四庫全書史部, 乾隆四十六年版, p.4a.

(7). "相" here is not "Prime Minister". Instead, it refers to "Ministerial Governor (侯國之相)", which held roughly the same administrative authority as a Governor (太守). See 班固,《漢書》Vol.9, 元帝紀. Hong Kong: 中華書局, 1970, p.283; 范曄,《後漢書》, 百官志. As in footnote (6), pp.3621-3622.

(8). 歐陽修,《集古錄》. As in footnote (6).

(9). Ibid..

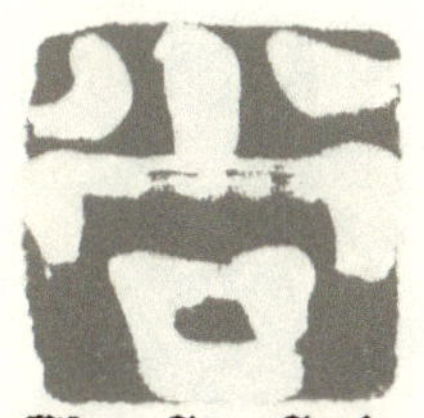

The SenSeis

尚尚齋